All Pam's Poems

All Pam's Poems
Pam Ayres

Illustrated by Roy Garnham Elmore

Hutchinson of London

Hutchinson & Co. (Publishers) Ltd
3 Fitzroy Square, London W1P 6JD

London Melbourne Sydney Auckland
Wellington Johannesburg and agencies
throughout the world

First published 1978
© Pam Ayres 1976, 1978

Drawings © Roy Garnham Elmore

Set in Century Schoolbook by Crawley Composition Ltd

Printed in Great Britain by the Anchor Press Ltd
and bound by Wm Brendon & Son Ltd,
both of Tiptree, Essex

ISBN 0 09 134380 1

For Mum and Dad with love

Contents

Poems continued:

Music:

The Poems...

Madbrains Watkins and his Travellin' Fair

Madbrains Watkins was his name,
He was a proper cove,
He had a little travellin' fair,
And the roundabout he drove.
He had to wind the handle,
Which he did at such a pace
That dobs of oil shot off the chain
And stuck upon your face.

There also was some hawkers
Who travelled with this fair,
One was a fat Italian maid
With a lot of hair.
She sold various confections,
From a little row of huts,
And hair got in the candyfloss
And on the monkey nuts.

Watkins had another job,
What he did unseen,
At the coconut shy,
Round behind a little screen.
He liked to see his coconuts,
Stuck on good and tight,
So he helped their staying power
With a little Araldite.

So you could fling them wooden balls
For all that you was worth,
But you would knock it clean in half
Before it hit the earth.
Then you might win a goldfish
In a plastic bag for free,
But the bag would have a puncture
And bowls was 90p.

There was a row of swinging boats,
And though the ropes was frayed,
Lots of kiddies went on it
And lots of kiddies paid.
And as their little fisties wrenched
The boats up in the air,
In his little office box,
Watkins knelt in prayer.

He had a little ghost train
Where he'd rush out in the gloom,
And as your train went rattlin' by,
He'd hit you with the broom.
Course, if it was old ladies
He had to take more care,
He'd either grab their knickers,
Or else he'd pull their hair.

He had a fortune teller,
But she only told for men,
Yet blokes went rushin' in that tent
Time and time again.
When she was tellin' fortunes,
A notice would appear,
Saying: "Don't spend all your money,
Back in half an hour, me dear."

So if you sees a travellin' fair
Come rattlin' down the track,
Make sure Madbrains Watkins
Is not grinnin' out the back.
Beware of Watkins' travellin' fair,
On lovely summer days,
Should he declare, "You'll walk on air,"
He means just what he says.

Sam and the Paraffin Man

Sam came home one evening,
The same as all his life,
To find the paraffin man
Had absconded with his wife.
Her coat from off the hanger
And her bootees from the stair
Had vanished, disappeared,
And furthermore, they were not there.

He came in through the kitchen,
The place was cold and still.
He tiptoed up the stairs,
In case his missis might be ill.
But nagging doubts they gathered,
Till what really did him in
Was, all across the landing,
He could smell the paraffin.

He took his knuckleduster
And he pressed it on his fist,
He also took a brick
In case the knuckleduster missed.
He set off down the darkened road,
Towards the caravan
Where he believed his missis
Hugged the paraffin man.

12

"Oh, the paraffin man, is it?"
Muttered Sam at every stride.
A little bird had told him
How the lorry stayed outside,
How all the neighbours down the street
Joined in the fun and games,
And said with all that oil,
Sam's house might well burst into flames.

He came upon the caravan,
His temper running riot,
But even he had to agree
The place was very quiet.
But then it quickly dawned on Sam,
This silence was a trick!
So he rushed up to the fanlight
And he hit it with a brick.

"Come out here with my missis!"
He bellowed at the door.
"I've heard about your lorry,
Parked outside two hours and more."
The caravan door opened
To reveal a woman's head,
And then a woman's nightdress,
For she'd just got out of bed.

She said, "I'm not the paraffin man,
But I am one of his daughters.
You look so worried, Sam,
Can I pour oil on troubled waters?"
She beckoned in the caravan
And Sam stepped up so quick.
Enraptured by her beauty,
He forgot to drop the brick.

Now unbeknown to Sam,
His faithless wife, she had not fled,
But with the paraffin man,
She was hiding in his shed.
She crept up to the window,
Though she had to kneel and crouch,
And saw her husband Samuel
Suffocating on the couch.

She took a pail of water
And she flung it in the door,
Just for to cool his ardour,
Only that and nothing more.
Too late she realised
That it was paraffin she threw,
And they all went up to Heaven
On a cloud of Esso Blue.

But on a winter's evening,
If your feet are less than quick,
You might smell an oily fragrance,
You might see a ghostly wick,
You might hear the distant rumble
Of a passing caravan,
For things that passion can't ignite,
Paraffin can.

Not you, Basil

Basil he loved Ethel,
  In his heart there burned a flame.
Every night he gripped the sheets
  And whispered Ethel's name,
He saw her every morning
  And the breath caught in his throat.
He loved her in her summer dress
  And in her winter coat.

Each night the lovely Ethel,
  She came to him in a dream,
And lay reclining in the boat
  He rowed them in, upstream.
Her hand trailed in the water
  And she was a wondrous sight,
Saying, "Basil! I can wait no more!
  Marry me, tonight!"

But his love was unrequited.
  When he saw her every day,
She only said, "How do,"
  And hurried past him on her way
To catch the bus to work,
  Where every day from morn to eve
She gazed out of the window,
  Thinking of her true love, Steve.

Now Steve he ran a scrapyard.
  Once a week he knocked the door
And Ethel, she would open it,
  Saying, "I know what you've come for!
Your rag and bones!" she cried,
  "And here they are, in this here sack,"
And she'd watch with heart a-flutter,
  As he heaved them on his back.

14

She never thought of Basil,
   Never knew that he was there.
From morn to eve, she thought of Steve,
   Her fingers, in his hair.
For Steve was rugged, like an oak,
   While Basil, like a skittle,
Had no physique, of which to speak,
   His muscles, they was little.

But his ardour never cooled
   And to himself he sadly said,
"If Ethel do not love me,
   Why, I'd just as soon be dead.
I'll knock upon her door,
   And say 'I love you' and forsooth,
She can either take or leave me,
   But at least I'll know the truth."

So he knocked upon her door
   And when she answered, he began:
"I know *someone* that you could make
   A Very Happy Man."
Ethel gripped the doorpost,
   "Do you mean Steve? Oh can it be?"
And Basil, looking at her,
   He said, "No, you fool, it's me."

She said, "Oh not *you*, Basil.
   I thought you'd come on Steve's behalf,
As though he'd see, a girl like me."
   (She laughed a tragic laugh)
She said, "I interrupted you,
   What were you going to say?"
And Basil said, "Don't matter,"
   And he coldly walked away.

Back in his house he primed his gun
   And placed it to his head,
"I die for Ethel, though my death'll
   Grieve her not," he said.
He strained to press the trigger,
   But his courage upped and fled,
So he rushed out in the garden
   And he shot the cat instead.

The Frogmarch

*This is a story about frogs who each year, in order to breed,
journey back to the pond in which they were hatched. To these
small creatures, motorways are a major obstacle.*

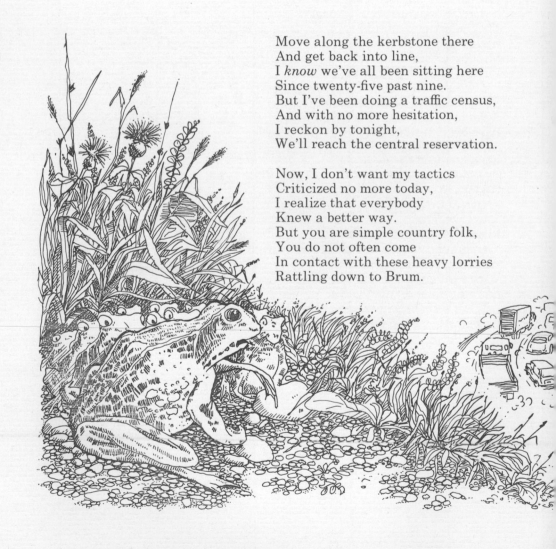

Move along the kerbstone there
And get back into line,
I *know* we've all been sitting here
Since twenty-five past nine.
But I've been doing a traffic census,
And with no more hesitation,
I reckon by tonight,
We'll reach the central reservation.

Now, I don't want my tactics
Criticized no more today,
I realize that everybody
Knew a better way.
But you are simple country folk,
You do not often come
In contact with these heavy lorries
Rattling down to Brum.

I know that when compared
To boggy riverbanks and peat,
That M40 motorway
Was murder on your feet.
I also know that in the usual
Places where we sit,
We don't stand up to find
Our underneath stuck up with grit.

Course, life for us amphibians
Is getting very harsh.
Take the Witney By-Pass,
It used to be a marsh.
They've irrigated all the land,
It's all gone to the dogs.
Mind, you get fantastic drainage,
But you don't get any frogs.

Still, keep your wits about you lads,
And before we're very much older,
We'll hop straight in the Promised Land,
And straight off this hard shoulder.
All the female frogs are there,
Tarting up the bower,
I'll give them that, they're very good,
That Sutton Coldfield shower.

Right then, watch the traffic,
'Cause I think I see a gap,
Wake old sleeping beauty up,
With his head sunk in his lap,
Get your bits and pieces then,
Is everybody there?
Look left! . . . Prepare to spring!
Oh, no . . . here comes St Giles's Fair.

Honey

My brother was, for many years,
  Apprenticed to the trade
Of building, and throughout that time
  A million bricks he laid.
He built a thousand dwellings
  In bricks of red and brown,
But sometimes, 'fore they built a house,
  They knocked the old one down.

On this partic'lar morning,
  With his companions bold,
He had to knock a house down
  That was decayed, and old.
The dreaded death-watch beetle,
  He didn't watch no more,
As me brother and his mates they
  Started tearing up the floor.

Well, the rafters and the tiling,
  It soon came rattling off,
Then the front door and the windows,
  While the dust it made them cough,
Till at last only the chimney
  Remained and stood intact,
And the others, to me brother said:
  "You knock that down, we're whacked."

Well, first he flexed his muscles,
  And then he flexed his neck,
Then he set about the chimney
  For to lay it on the deck.
He bashed it in the fireplace,
  And he bashed it in the grate,
And he bashed a bloke stood watchin'
  'Cause he saw him just too late.

But as the fireplace crumbled,
  He was surprised to see
What come buzzing, panic-stricken,
  Out in front of him, a bee.
And where the bricks had fell away
  Was where it had its home,
For all lined up the chimney
  Was a great big honeycomb.

And lovely golden honey,
  It came rolling down the wall,
All in the dust and rubbish
  And the fag ends there and all,
He could not see it go to waste.
  He put the honeycomb
Into a rubber bucket
  And he took the bucket home.

Now Mother, she was took aback,
  While staring in the bucket.
"Why thank you dear," she said surprised,
  "All I can say is what luck it
Was you that knocked the chimney down,
  And brought this home to me.
We'll hang it somewhere warm,
  So's it drips out, in time for tea."

So in the airing cupboard it was hung
  With bits of string,
And honey ran into the pan,
  She'd put to catch it in,
It dripped upon the folded sheets,
  And Dad's pants on the rack,
So when he put them on next day,
  They stuck all down his back.

contd.

But oh, it was a luxury,
  With honey on our bread.
When Mother shouted: "Whadya want?"
  "Honey, please," we said.
And in the heated cupboard,
  It gathered in the pan.
As though there was no end to it,
  Out the honey ran.

But, alas! 'twas our misfortune,
  As we found out next day,
We was not the only ones,
  Knew where the honey lay.
Mother, in the morning,
  Went to fetch some for the house
And found all drownded in the pan,
  Upside down, a mouse!

The honey gummed his whiskers
  And his fur was stuck up tight.
To add insult on to injury,
  He'd messed in it, from fright.
Mother, with the jam jar,
  She stood at the cupboard door
Saying, "Go and fetch your father,
  There's no honey any more."

Father he ran up so fast,
  His roll-up fell apart,
Saying, "I told you not to put it there!
  I told you, from the start!
I told you we'd get vermin,
  And didn't we get them quick,
Oh, chuck it in the dustbin,
  'Cause it's making me feel sick!"

And so the lovely honeycomb
  Got bundled out the door,
We all went back to Marmite
  Which we used to have before.
My brother searched in vain
  Up every flue his head he put
But he didn't find no more honey
  All he ever found was soot.

The Bunny Poem

I am a bunny rabbit
Sitting in me hutch.
I like to sit up this end,
I don't care for that end much.
I'm glad tomorrow's Thursday,
'Cause with a bit of luck,
As far as I remember
That's the day they pass the buck.

Oh, I Wish I'd looked after me Teeth

Oh, I wish I'd looked after me teeth,
  And spotted the perils beneath
All the toffees I chewed,
  And the sweet sticky food.
Oh, I wish I'd looked after me teeth.

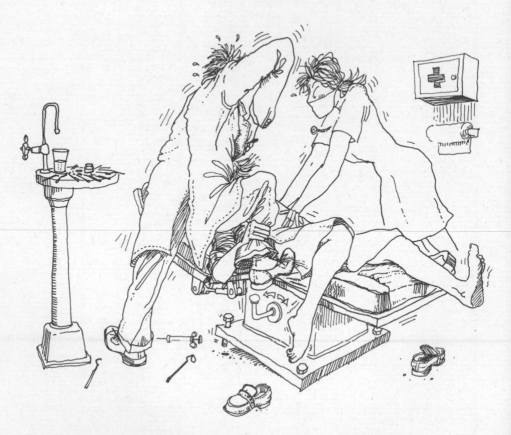

I wish I'd been that much more willin'
  When I had more tooth there than fillin'
To pass up gobstoppers,
  From respect to me choppers,
And to buy something else with me shillin'.

When I think of the lollies I licked
  And the liquorice allsorts I picked,
Sherbet dabs, big and little,
  All that hard peanut brittle,
My conscience gets horribly pricked.

My mother, she told me no end,
  "If you got a tooth, you got a friend."
I was young then, and careless,
  My toothbrush was hairless,
I never had much time to spend.

Oh I showed them the toothpaste all right,
  I flashed it about late at night,
But up-and-down brushin'
  And pokin' and fussin'
Didn't seem worth the time – I could bite!

If I'd known I was paving the way
  To cavities, caps and decay,
The murder of fillin's,
  Injections and drillin's,
I'd have thrown all me sherbet away.

So I lay in the old dentist's chair,
  And I gaze up his nose in despair,
And his drill it do whine
  In these molars of mine.
"Two amalgam," he'll say, "for in there."

How I laughed at my mother's false teeth,
  As they foamed in the waters beneath.
But now comes the reckonin'
  It's *me* they are beckonin'
Oh, I *wish* I'd looked after me teeth.

In Fear of the Butcher

There is an art which ladies have
With which I can't compete,
And that's the art of knowing
How to pick out joints of meat.
It must be very nice to know
Your sirloin from your rump,
Or if you get a better bet
With brisket than with chump.

You see, me being single,
I never have to care,
A plate of beans and bangers
Will keep me from despair.
But when I have my friends in,
That's when I come unstuck,
That's when I brave the butcher
And go to try me luck.

I stand there in the butcher's queue
With courage screwed and mustered.
But when I hear, "Yes please, dear?"
That's when I get all flustered,
That's when I wish I really knew
Me scrag end from me hock,
Me belly from me chitlins,
And me knees they start to knock.

He says, "A pound of steak, dear?"
(I hates him and he knows.it)
Or else he'll say, "A chicken?
Here's a fresh one but we froze it,"
While all the ladies in the queue
Are shuffling of their feet.
My friends! It is a nightmare
When I buy a piece of meat.

And every single time I say,
"I'll have a bit of that!"
Pointing wildly at the window
And a great big lump of fat.
Oh, all you other ladies,
I don't know how you do it,
How you acquire what you desire
And not a lump of suet.

I'll be a vegetarian
All gnawing at an apple,
No more with talk of lamb and pork
Will I have to grapple.
And if my friends they visit me,
I'll look them in the eye,
And if they've come to dinner
Well, I'll tell them . . . Good-bye!

I'm a Starling... me Darling

We're starlings, the missis, meself and the boys.
We don't go round hoppin', we walks,
We don't go in for this singing all day
And twittering about, we just squawks.

We don't go in for these fashionable clothes
Like old Missel Thrush, and his spots,
Me breast isn't red, there's no crest on me head,
We've got sort of, hardwearing . . . dots.

We starlings, the missis, meself and the boys,
We'll eat anything that's about,
Well, anything but that old half coconut,
I can't hold it still. I falls out.

What we'd rather do is wait here for you
To put out some bread for the tits,
And then when we're certain you're there by the curtain,
We flocks down and tears it to bits.

But we starlings, the missis, meself and the boys,
We reckon that we're being got at.
You think for two minutes, them finches and linnets,
You never sees them being shot at.

So the next time you comes out to sprinkle the crumbs out,
And there's starlings there, making a noise,
Don't you be so quick to heave half a brick,
It's the missis, meself and the boys!

In Defence of Hedgehogs

I am very fond of hedgehogs
Which makes me want to say
That I am struck with wonder
How there's any left today.
For each morning as I travel,
And no short distance that,
All I see are hedgehogs,
Squashed. And dead. And flat.

Now, hedgehogs are not clever,
No, hedgehogs are quite dim
And when he sees your headlamps,
Well, it don't occur to him
That the very wisest thing to do
Is up and run away.
No! he curls up in a stupid ball
And no doubt starts to pray.

Well, motor cars do travel
At a most alarming rate,
And by the time you sees him,
It is very much too late.
And thus he gets a-squasho'd,
Unrecorded but for me,
With me pen and paper,
Sittin' in a tree.

It is statistically proven,
In chapter and in verse,
That in a car-and-hedgehog fight,
The hedgehog comes off worse.
When whistlin' down your prop shaft,
And bouncin' off your diff,
His coat of nice brown prickles
Is not effect-iff.

A hedgehog cannot make you laugh,
Whistle, dance or sing,
And he ain't much to look at,
And he don't make anything,
And in amongst his prickles,
There's fleas and bugs and that,
But there ain't no need to leave him,
Squashed. And dead. And flat.

Oh, spare a thought for hedgehogs,
Spare a thought for me,
Spare a thought for hedgehogs,
As you drink your cup of tea,
Spare a thought for hedgehogs,
Hoverin' on the brinkt,
Spare a thought for hedgehogs,
Lest they become extinct.

Let's all Strut to the Lifeguard's Hut

It was on the beach at Newquay,
  I was struttin' up and down,
With me bathing suit unbuttoned,
  In the hopes of getting brown.
The icy wind it chilled me
  And the rain washed o'er me face,
But I strutted up and down, lads,
  And I never changed me pace.

'Twas then I saw the lifeguard!
  Lyin' flat upon the deck,
A crowd of nubile women
  Hanging on his words. And neck.
I said, "Oh how disgustin',
  Has the man got no decorum?"
For I'd have took his eye, lads,
  If I'd just got there beforum.

I strutted on the shingle
   And I strutted on the sand,
I strutted in the ocean
   And I strutted on the land,
I strutted through the café
   And I strutted down the rock,
But when it came to struttin' back,
   'Twas then I got a shock.

I had strutted out too far, lads,
   And got cut off by the tide,
I could not strut back up the rock
   Nor yet strut round the side,
I could not strut upon the ocean
   For sure I could not float,
And 'twas then I saw the lifeguard,
   Fast approaching in his boat.

I put my hands up to my mouth
   And loudly I did call,
As I undid all me swimsuit,
   Rolling up the sleeves and all,
The lifeguard, on the quarterdeck,
   Cried reassuring things
As he stood beside the tops'l,
   Blowing up his water wings.

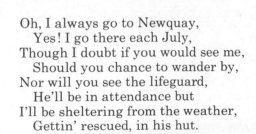

Oh, I always go to Newquay,
   Yes! I go there each July,
Though I doubt if you would see me,
   Should you chance to wander by,
Nor will you see the lifeguard,
   He'll be in attendance but
I'll be sheltering from the weather,
   Gettin' rescued, in his hut.

Like you Would

Well, I got up in the morning,
Like you would.
And I cooked a bit of breakfast,
Like you would.
But at the door I stopped,
For a message had been dropped,
And I picked it up, and read it,
Like you would.

"Oh, Blimey!" I said,
Like you would.
"Have a read of this,
This is good!"
It said: "I live across the way,
And admire you every day,
And my heart, it breaks without you."
Well, it would.

It said: "I'd buy you furs and jewels,
If I could.
And I go along with that,
I think he should.
It said: "Meet me in the park,
When it's good and dark,
And so me wife won't see,
I'll wear a hood."

Oh, I blushed with shame and horror,
Like you would.
That a man would ask me that,
As if I could!
So I wrote him back a letter,
Saying, "No, I think it's better
If I meet you in the Rose and Crown,
Like we did last Thursday."

Sling another Chair Leg on the Fire, Mother

Sling another chair leg on the fire, Mother,
Pull your orange box up to the blaze,
Hold your poor old mittens out and warm them
In these inflationary days.
Sink your teeth into that dripping sandwich,
Flick the telly on to channel nine,
And if we get the sound without the picture,
Well, I'll kick it in the kidneys, one more time.

Come with me out to the empty garage,
We haven't been there for a week or more,
We'll bow our heads and gaze in silent homage
At the spots of oil upon the floor.
We'll think of when we had a motor car there,
Which used to take us out in rain or shine,
Before the price of petrol went beyond us,
And we'll make believe we kept it, one more time.

Fling another sausage in the pan, Mother!
We'll laugh away our worries and our cares,
But we'll never get a doctor after hours, Mother,
So for God's sake don't go falling down the stairs.
Toss another lentil in the soup, Mother!
And serve it up before the News at nine,
And if the GPO detector spots us,
Make believe we've got a licence, one more time.

There was a time we'd booked up for Ibiza,
We'd bought the suntan lotion and the clothes,
But we never got beyond the travel agent,
'Cause Court Line organized the one we chose.
So knock the clouds of dust from off the brochure,
Wipe the 40-watt bulb free of grime,
Turn the dog-eared pages to Ibiza,
And we'll make believe we got there, one more time.

Pass me the hatchet and the axe, Mother!
Wipe away that sad and anxious frown,
What with these inflationary spirals,
It's *nice* to see the table falling down.
Your poor old shins will soon be good and mottled,
Once the flames get round that teak veneer,
And in the ring of warm and dancing firelight,
We'll smile and wish each other: Happy New Year.

The Battery Hen

Oh, I am a battery hen,
On me back there's not a germ,
I never scratched a farmyard,
And I never pecked a worm.
I never had the sunshine
To warm me feathers through.
Eggs I lay. Every day.
For the likes of you.

When you has them scrambled,
Piled up on your plate,
It's me what you should thank for that.
I never lays them late,
I always lays them reg'lar,
I always lays them right,
I never lays them brown,
I always lays them white.

But it's no life for a battery hen.
In me box I'm sat,
A funnel stuck out from the side,
Me pellets comes down that.
I gets a squirt of water,
Every half a day,
Watchin' with me beady eye,
Me eggs roll away.

I lays them in a funnel,
Strategically placed
So that I don't kick 'em
And let them go to waste.
They rolls off down the tubing
And up the gangway quick,
Sometimes I gets to thinkin',
"That could have been a chick!"

I might have been a farmyard hen,
Scratchin' in the sun,
There might have been a crowd of chicks,
After me to run.
There might have been a cockerel fine
To pay us his respects,
Instead of sittin' here,
Till someone comes and wrings our necks.

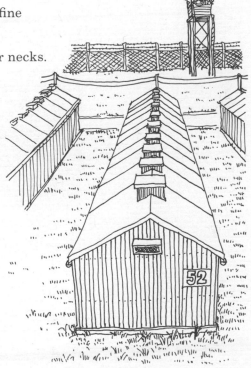

I see the Time and Motion clock
Is sayin' nearly noon.
I 'spec me squirt of water
Will come flyin' at me soon,
And then me spray of pellets
Will nearly break me leg,
And I'll bite the wire nettin'
And lay one more bloody egg.

The Hegg

A thrush, disconsolate, with no sign of a mate,
Sat morbidly perched in a tree,
Saying, "I tell the tale
Of a flighty young male,
Who have done the dirty on me.

"I'm Hexpecting a Hegg, a Hillicit Hegg,
A Hegg lyeth here, in my breast.
While the trees were bright-leaved
I rashly conceived
A Hegg, Houtside of the Nest.

"For my deed I am shunned, and left moribund,
And by all I am left on a limb.
I would give my right wing,
To be rid of this thing,
And for my great girth to be slim."

Just then a black crow, with his black eyes a-glow,
Boldly down to the thrush flew,
Said, "The grapevine, I've heard,
Tells of a distressed bird,
Which I've reason to think may be you."

He stood on one leg, said, "You're having an Egg
And the other birds feel you are bad.
But if with me you came,
You'd be free of the shame,
Of having an Egg with no Dad.

"For a nominal fee, I will take you to see
My friend, who lives up the back doubles.
If you swear not to fail
To pay on the nail,
He will duff up the source of your troubles!"

So the thrush, unafraid, assented and paid,
And went under cover of night
To see an old Bustard, with gin and with mustard,
And to be relieved of her plight.

She was made to sit in a bathful of gin,
And she was obliging and meek.
She was made to consume
Some soap and a prune,
And her feathers fell out for a week.

Outside on the bough, she said, "Look at me now,
Of my Hegg I am freed, but I'm Hill,
And if Hagain I stray
Without naming the day
Then first I shall go on the Pill."

Pam Ayres and the Embarrassing Experience with the Parrot

At the Cotswold Wild Life Park,
In the merry month of May,
I paid the man the money,
And went in to spend the day.
Straightway to the Pets Corner
I turned my eager feet,
To go and see the rabbits
And give them something to eat.

As I approached the hutches,
I was alarmed to see
A crowd of little yobbos,
'Ollerin' with glee.
I crept up close behind them
And weighed the scene up quick,
And saw them poke the rabbits
Poke them! . . . with a stick!

"Get off you little buggers!"
I shouted in their ear.
"Don't you poke them rabbits,
That's not why they are here."
I must have really scared them,
In seconds they were gone,
And feelin' I had done some good,
I carried on along.

Till up beside the Parrots Cage,
I stood to view the scene.
They was lovely parrots,
Beautiful blue and green,
In and out the nestbox,
They was really having fun,
Squawking out and flying about,
All except for one.

One poor old puffed-up parrot
Clung grimly to his perch,
And as the wind blew frontwards,
Backwards he would lurch.
One foot up in his feathers,
Abandoned by the rest,
He sat there, plainly dying,
His head upon his chest.

Well, I walked on down the pathway
And I stroked a nanny goat,
But the thought of parrots dyin'
Brought a lump into me throat.
I could no longer stand it
And to the office I fled.
Politely I began: "S'cuse me,
Your parrot's nearly dead."

So me and a curator,
In urgent leaps and bounds,
With a bottle of Parrot Cure,
Dashed across the grounds.
The dust flew up around us
As we reached the Parrots Pen,
And the curator he turned to me,
Saying, "Which one is it then?"

You know what I am going to say:
He was not there at all,
At least, not where I left him.
No, he flit from wall to wall,
As brightly as a button
Did he squawk and jump and leap.
The curator was very kind,
Saying, "I expect he was asleep."

But I was humiliated
As I stood before the wire.
The curator went back
To put his feet up by the fire,
So I let the parrot settle,
And after a short search,
I found the stick the yobbos had,
And poked him off his perch.

The Stuffed Horse

There was a stuffed horse what had died,
And the townspeople stood it with pride
On a plinth in the Square,
And the shoppers went there,
And sat, for a rest, by its side.

Beneath the stuffed horse was a plaque,
Only vandals had painted it black,
What told of the deed
Of the glorious steed,
And the General, what rode on its back.

The bold horse, with never a care,
Had ducked cannonballs in the air,
And stood to the end
By the General, his friend,
Which was why he was put in the Square.

Well, his tail it was stuck out with wire,
And paint made his nostrils afire,
And his bold eye of glass
Gazed upon concrete grass,
When he met with his fate, what was dire.

This night from the shadows a-fidget
Extended a beckonin' digit.
A voice whispered, "Right,"
And into the night
Rushed ten men, a saw and a midget.

They lay by the horse with no word,
And the soft sound of sawing was heard.
In silence, all night,
Stuffin' flew left and right,
And into a sack was transferred.

When the church clock struck quarter to four,
Ten men ran away, and a saw.
But the midget, my friend,
Was not there at the end,
He was with his companions no more.

When morning it broke on the Square,
You would never have known they'd been there,
For the horse gazed away,
Like the previous day,
Just sniffin' the spring in the air.

But walkin' across to the spot
Came two ladies whose feet had grown hot.
They sat on the ground,
And one got out a pound,
Saying: "Here's that quid I owed to you, Dot."

From the back of the stuffed horse's throat
Came a hand and it snatched the pound note.
With the hand, and the cash,
The jaws shut with a clash,
And the horse gazed away with a gloat.

contd.

The lady was helped off to bed.
"I thought they liked hay, dear," she said.
No one listened, of course,
For it was a stuffed horse
What never required to be fed.

But it happened again, the next day,
When a vicar had sat down to pray.
He said, "Lord, bless my flock,"
When a great lead-filled sock
Took his senses, and wallet, away.

But by now the long arm of the law
Started pickin' up pieces of straw,
What might have been nothin'
But could have been stuffin'.
And random observers, they saw.

That the stuffed horse's eye, though of glass,
Had seemed to be watchin' them pass
And sometimes would blink
Or give you a wink,
As if to say, "Step on my grass."

Hadrian of the Yard, he was called,
He was like Fabian, only bald.
He said, "I'll be an idiot,
If there's not a midgiot
Inside of the stuffed horse installed."

And indeed, that great sleuth, he was right.
By Caesarean, they caught him that night,
With ten men and a saw.
He had broken the law
Illegal entry, all right.

But tragic indeed was the scene
In the place where the stuffed horse had been.
Bandy-legged and defaced,
He had to be replaced,
By an ordinary bust of the Queen.

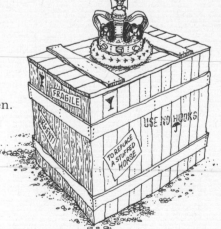

The Curlers Poem

A set of heated rollers
Is every maid's delight.
It stops you wearing curlers
In the middle of the night.
It keeps you looking spick and span,
When all the rest are not,
And though your hands are freezing cold,
Your head is nice and hot.

In Favour of
Pushing your Car over a Cliff
and Buying a Bike

I am a mighty garage
On the corner of the Square,
And it is all my pleasure
To provide a quick repair,
Or I can do your service
In the blinking of an eye.
I wouldn't say it's thorough,
But it'll get you by.

If you break down, we might tow you in,
I suppose that's what we're for.
Despite the astronomic bill,
It's still a bloody chore.
We'll glare beneath your bonnet,
And we'll reel it off so pat,
Did you know that needs replacing?
And that? And that? And that?

Or we might buy your little car,
For half of what it's worth,
After we've convinced you
It's got every fault on earth.
But pass me by and presto!
In the window it'll be
As Clean! One Owner! Spotless!
And the price tag that you see

Will bear no fond resemblance
To the price in our demands,
When we said how much we'd give you
Just to take it off your hands.
The price will strangely rocket,
And the things we said were wrong,
Without help from the mechanics
Are conveniently gone!

But when the next poor muggins,
He comes looking for a car,
And asks a few odd questions,
They won't get him very far.
We don't say the sub-frame's rotten,
Or the whining from the rear
Is out of the back axle,
And not ringing in his ear.

For I'm such a busy garage
And my memory is short,
I don't want people trusting me
Or troubles of that sort.
We don't want you dissenters,
Butting into our sales pitch,
We just sit here, on the corner,
Growing big. And fat. And rich.

Goodwill to Men: Give us your Money

It was Christmas Eve on a Friday,
   The shops was full of cheer,
With tinsel in the windows,
   And presents twice as dear.
A thousand Father Christmases
   Sat in their little huts,
And folk was buying crackers
   And folk was buying nuts.

All up and down the country,
   Before the light was snuffed,
Turkeys they got murdered,
   And cockerels they got stuffed.
Christmas cakes got marzipanned,
   And puddin's they got steamed,
Mothers they got desperate,
   And tired kiddies screamed.

Hundredweights of Christmas cards
   Went flying through the post,
With first-class postage stamps on those
   You had to flatter most.
Within a million kitchens,
   Mince pies was being made,
On everybody's radio,
   "White Christmas", it was played.

48

Out in the frozen countryside,
   Men crept round on their own,
Hacking off the holly
   What other folks had grown,
Mistletoe in willow trees
   Was by a man wrenched clear,
So he could kiss his neighbour's wife
   He'd fancied all the year.

And out upon the hillside
   Where the Christmas trees had stood,
All was completely barren
   But for little stumps of wood.
The little trees that flourished
   All the year were there no more,
But in a million houses
   Dropped their needles on the floor.

And out of every cranny, cupboard,
   Hiding place and nook,
Little bikes and kiddies' trikes
   Were secretively took.
Yards of wrapping paper
   Was rustled round about,
And bikes were wheeled to bedrooms
   With the pedals sticking out.

Rolled up in Christmas paper,
   The Action Men were tensed,
All ready for the morning,
   When their fighting life commenced.
With tommy guns and daggers,
   All clustered round about,
"Peace on Earth – Goodwill to Men",
   The figures seemed to shout.

The church was standing empty,
   The pub was standing packed,
There came a yell, "Noel, Noel!"
   And glasses they got cracked.
From up above the fireplace,
   Christmas cards began to fall,
And trodden on the floor, said:
   "Merry Xmas, to you all."

Oh no, I got a Cold

I am sitting on the sofa
By the fire and staying in,
Me head is free of comfort
And me nose is free of skin.
Me friends have run for cover,
They have left me pale and sick
With me pockets full of tissues
And me nostrils full of Vick.

That bloke in the telly adverts,
He's supposed to have a cold.
He has a swig of whatnot
And he drops off, good as gold,
His face like snowing harvest
Slips into sweet repose.
Well, I bet this tortured breathing
Never whistled down his nose.

I burnt me bit of dinner
'Cause I've lost me sense of smell,
But then, I couldn't taste it,
So that worked out very well.
I'd buy some, down the café
But I know that at the till
A voice from work will softly say,
"I thought that you were ill."

So I'm wrapped up in a blanket
With me feet up on a stool,
I've watched the telly programmes
And the kids come home from school.
But what I haven't watched for
Is any sympathy,
'Cause all you ever get is:
"Oh no, keep away from me!"

Medicinal discovery,
It moves in mighty leaps,
It leapt straight past the common cold
And gave it us for keeps.
Now I'm not a fussy woman,
There's no malice in me eye,
But I wish that they could cure
the common cold. That's all. Good-bye.

The Spot Welder's Dream

I wish I was a pop star,
Colourful and brash,
With me earoles full of crochets
And me wallet full of cash.
To hide me bit of acne
I'll stick sequins on me face,
Then I can do the vocals
And you can do the base.
Yeah.

I can do the vocals,
But to whip them to a frenzy,
Seated at the organ,
We'll have rockin' Bert McKenzie.
Now Bert's a lovely mover
But he tends to be a dunce,
When he's winking at the boppers,
He shuts both eyes at once.

I'll buy a cossack shirt
Split to the waist, in peacock red,
So me face will get them going
And me chest will knock them dead.
I'll wave me great long legs about
And wrap them round the mike.
I had a practice Saturday,
But I fell off me bike.

I'll get meself an agent
And a manager and all,
A bloke to drive the minibus,
And one to book the hall,
A musical arranger,
And a private record plugger,
So when we're in the charts,
Well, we shall all feel that much smugger.

And when we're doing a stand,
I'll come up quiet, to the mike,
I'll stick me pelvis out,
And say, "Right on . . ." suggestive like.
I'll drive the women crazy,
They'll be in such a state.
And they'll scratch each other's eyes out,
Once I've had me teeth put straight.

Farewell Cradley Heath!
We're out upon the road to fame.
Farewell factory gates!
We're going to be a Household Name.
Good riddance Welding Shop,
And factory hooter every morn,
For it's me and Bert McKenzie,
A Superstar is born.

I am a Cunnin' Vending Machine

I am a cunnin' vending machine
Lurkin' in the hall,
So you can't kick me delicate parts
I'm bolted to the wall.
Come on! Drop in your money,
Don't let's hang about,
I'll do my level best to see
You don't get nothing out.

I sees you all approachin',
The fagless and the dry,
All fumblin' in your pockets,
And expectant in the eye.
I might be in your place of work,
Or on the High Street wall.
Trust in me! In theory,
I cater for you all.

Within these windows I provide
For every human state,
Hunger, night starvation,
And remembering birthdays late.
Just read the information,
Pop the money in - that's grand,
And I'll see absolutely nothing
Ever drops down in your hand.

I might be at your swimming bath,
And you'd come, cold and wet,
With a shilling in your hand,
Some hot soup for to get.
And as you stand in wet
Anticipation of a sup,
I will dispense the soup,
But I will not dispense the cup.

And then it's all-out war,
Because you lost your half-a-nicker.
Mighty kicks and blows with bricks
Will make me neon flicker,
But if you bash me up,
So I'm removed, me pipes run dry,
There's no way you can win,
I'll send me brother by and by.

Once there was friendly ladies,
Years and years before,
Who stood with giant teapots,
Saying, "What can I do you for?"
They'd hand you all the proper change,
And pour your cup of tea,
But they're not economic so . . .
Hard luck! You're stuck with me.

I am a ...

I am a Witney Blanket,
Original and Best.
You'll never get cold feet
With me across your chest.

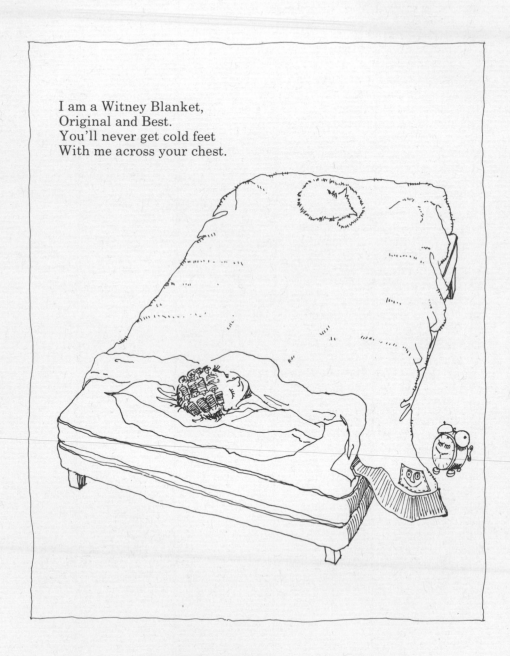

I am a ...

I am a Dry Stone Waller,
All day I Dry Stone Wall.
Of all appalling callings,
Dry Stone Walling's
Worst of all.

Little
Lawrence
Greenaway

Little Lawrence Greenaway,
He tended to digress.
He'd always tell you rather more
Instead of rather less.
Of wild exaggeration
He was never known to tire,
The facts became irrelevant,
In short, he was a liar.

He said, "I'm in computers,
You name the sort, we've gottem,"
Whereas in fact he only
Screwed the castors on the bottom.
His claims they grew preposterous,
He couldn't understand
Why all of his companions,
Well, they laughed behind their hands.

One awful Monday morning,
He was sitting on the train,
He saw a great red-headed man
Come rushing down the lane.
Just as the train was leaving,
The man wrenched at the door
And stood above the passengers,
A mighty six foot four.

He opened up his great big mouth
And with a ghastly shout,
Hollered, "Somewhere on this train's
The bloke who took my Missis out!"
Lawrence he was frightened,
Like a frightened rabbit,
But he still said, "It was me,"
You see, just through force of habit.

The great big man, he picked him up
Underneath the throat,
And helped him off the train,
Without returning for his coat.
With his head locked in a headlock
He was rushed off down the lane,
And little Lawrence Greenaway,
He were *never seen again.*

Walk with me for a Perch and a Rood

I don't want metrication, friends,
The milligramme and litre,
I work in feet and inches,
I do not trust the metre.
I cannot calculate it,
I don't know where I am,
Give me half a hundredweight
And you can have a gramme.

Metrication? I can't learn it,
I am too long in the tooth,
My schooldays they are over,
Gorn! with the bloom of youth.
I work in tenths of inches,
The furlong and the chain,
The rood and pole, the six-foot hole,
I like it nice and plain.

I like it by the furlong,
And I like it by the acre,
I liked the baker's dozen,
And I also liked the baker.
I liked the bushel basket,
And a peck's alright by me,
Them metrics put the prices up
As far as I can see.

I didn't want the decimals,
I don't want metrication,
I wouldn't know a litre
If you poured it in a basin.
I'll have my pints and gallons
As long as I am able,
My glass I'll fill with a sixth of a gill,
And I'll see you under the table!

The Dolly on the Dustcart

I'm the dolly on the dustcart,
I can see you're not impressed,
I'm fixed above the driver's cab,
With wire across me chest,
The dustman see, he spotted me,
Going in the grinder,
And he fixed me on the lorry,
I dunno if that was kinder.

This used to be a lovely dress,
In pink and pretty shades,
But it's torn now, being on the cart,
And black as the ace of spades,
There's dirt all round me face,
And all across me rosy cheeks,
Well, I've had me head thrown back,
But we ain't had no rain for weeks.

I used to be a 'Mama' doll,
Tipped forward, I'd say 'Mum'
But the rain got in me squeaker,
And now I been struck dumb,
I had two lovely blue eyes,
But out in the wind and weather,
One's sunk back in me head like,
And one's gone altogether.

I'm not a soft, flesh coloured dolly,
Modern children like so much,
I'm one of those hard old dollies,
What are very cold to touch,
Modern dolly's underwear,
Leaves me a bit nonplussed,
I haven't got a bra,
But then I haven't got a bust!

Yet I was happy in that dolls house,
I was happy as a Queen,
I never knew that Tiny Tears,
Was coming on the scene,
I heard of dolls with hair that grew,
And I was quite enthralled,
Until I realised *my* head
Was hard and pink . . . and bald.

So I travels with the rubbish,
Out of fashion, out of style,
Out of me environment,
For mile after mile,
No longer prized . . . dustbinized!
Unfeminine, Untidy,
I'm the dolly on the dustcart.
There'll be no collection Friday.

Where There's a Will

... there's a sobbing relation

All the family was gathered
To hear poor Grandad's will,
Fred was watching Alice,
And she was watching Bill.
He was watching Arthur,
Everywhere he went,
But specially at the cupboard,
Where Grandad kept the rent.

Outside on the patio,
The sliding door was closed,
And sitting in a chair
Was nephew John, his face composed.
He said, "Me dear old Grandad,
I shall never see you more,"
And his sheets of calculations
Were spread across the floor.

Downstairs in the kitchen,
Sister Alice blew her nose,
Saying, "He always was my favourite,
You *knew* that I suppose?
You couldn't have found a nicer man,
I've never loved one dearer.
I'd have come round *much* more often
If I'd lived just that bit nearer.

Cousin Arthur sat alone
His eyes were wild and rash,
And desperately he tried to think
Where old folks hid their cash.
He'd thought about the armchair
And the mattress on the bed,
And he'd left his car at home
And booked a Pickford's van instead.

Then there were the bedroom floorboards
He'd studied every crack,
And twice, while dusting the commode,
He'd rolled the carpet back.
But he knew the others watched him
"You scavengers," he cursed,
And every night he prayed,
"Don't let the others find it first."

The day that Grandad's will was read,
It came up bright and clear,
The solicitor looked round,
And said, "Now then, are we all here?"
Someone shouted, "Yes",
And someone else unscrewed his pen,
And someone sat upon his coat,
So he could not stand up again.

He carefully unfolded it
And wonderingly said,
"This is the shortest will
I ever will have read."
He rolled a fag and carefully
Laid in a filter tip,
While beads of sweat they gathered
On Cousin Arthur's lip.

It says: "Me dear relations,
Thank you all for being so kind,
And out beside the lily pond
You will surely find
The half a million pounds,
With which I stuffed me garden gnome,
Which I leave, with great affection,
To the Battersea Dogs' Home."

All about Pumpkins

In this part of Oxfordshire, pumpkin-growing competitions are very popular. In the spring, all contestants receive a seed from the same pumpkin. The heaviest pumpkin from the plants reared is the winner. For one such weigh-in, a tense occasion at Bampton, I was asked to present the prize and come up with a suitable poem. Here it is.

I've been asked here this evening
To congratulate the winner,
And also to encourage both
The novice and beginner.
If your pumpkins are a problem,
And you never win a prize,
A little of the following
Is what I would advise.

When you get your pumpkin seed,
Don't drop it on the ground.
First, make sure that it is oval,
It's a tater if it's round.
And if your neighbour accidentally
Drops his by your shoe,
Make good and sure you stamp on it,
Then say it wasn't you.

Don't do the seed with Derris
Or any fancy stuff.
Take it from your pocket,
Dusting off the bits of fluff,
And wait until it's dark
Before you go to bury it,
So no saboteur can come
And shower it with Flit.

And when you are a-digging
And turning of the sod,
Watch out where you put your boots,
Or on it you have trod.
Don't put a bucket over
To make it long and white,
For when you take the bucket off,
It will fall down with fright.

But if the worst should happen,
And nextdoor's makes yours look small,
Here's your course of action,
'Cause that won't do at all.
You *could* bash theirs with a mallet,
But they'd suspect at once,
You've got to it cunning,
It makes all the differ unce.

You takes hold of your pumpkin,
And this is cheating but
The circumstance demands it,
And you makes a little cut,
Somewhere in the pumpkin,
In the front or in the back,
And you takes a great big lump of lead
And stuffs it in the crack.

So when they put it on the scales,
Right before your eyes
The needle will go whizzing round,
And you will win the prize,
Ignore the shouts of "Crooked!"
And scorn the cries of "Bent!"
Lead lining in your pumpkin
Lends weight to your argument.

Puddings - A Slice of Nostalgia

Don't open no more tins of Irish Stew, Alice,
You know it makes me pace the bedroom floor,
You gave me Irish Stew a week last Sunday,
And I never got to sleep till half past four,
You open up another tin of spam, Alice,
Or them frankfurter sausages in brine,
And we'll stab them, sitting opposite each other,
And you can dream your dreams, and I'll dream mine.

I'll dream about me apple cheeked old mother,
Her smiling face above a pot of broth,
She used to cook us every kind of pudding,
Proper puddings . . . in a pudding cloth!
When we came home from school all cold and hungry.
One look along the clothes line was enough,
And if the pudding cloth was there a-flapping,
We all knew what it meant—a suet duff!

A suet duff would set your cheeks a-glowing,
Suet duff and custard, in a mound,
And even if you'd run about all morning,
A suet duff would stick you to the ground,
Or else there'd be a lovely batter pudding,
With all the edges baked so hard and black,
So if your teeth had grown a bit too long like,
Well, that would be the stuff to grind them back.

She used to make us lovely apple puddings,
She'd boil them all the morning on the stove,
If you bit on something hard that wasn't apple,
The chances were, you'd bitten on a clove,
Or else there'd be a great jam roly poly,
We'd watch it going underneath the knife,
And if you took a bite a bit too early,
The red hot jam would scar your mouth for life.

Oh bring back the roly poly pudding,
Bread and butter pudding . . . Spotted Dick!
Great big jugs full up of yellow custard,
That's the sort of pudding I would pick,
But here's the tube of artificial cream, Alice,
I've cleaned the nozzle out, the hole's so fine,
And we'll squirt it on our little pots of yoghurt,
And you can dream your dreams, and I'll dream mine.

The Sea Shell

Don't 'ee fret no more, my darlin' Alice,
Don't 'ee cry and sorrow, my old dear,
Don't 'ee watch the lane for our son Arnold,
Lost upon the sea this fourteen year.
Let a smile play on your lips again, Alice,
Fourteen years you've worn the widows drab,
And get your ear away from that great sea shell:
Nobody hears the ocean in a crab.

How I Loved You, Ethel Preedy, with Your Neck so Long and Slender

How I loved you, Ethel Preedy,
With your neck so long and slender.
At the Tennis Dance
What magic charm did you engender!
Our eyes met in the crowd,
Your fingers tightened on the racquet,
But when I tore my gaze away
Some swine pinched me jacket.

The Baby Shop

There is a Baby Shop, at the corner of the street,
Where all sorts of people coincidentally meet,
Some who cannot do it, and some who've lost the knack,
And those who do not want to, and them with a bad back.

But you can buy a baby there of any shape or size,
They do them up with blue or green or brown or hazel eyes
So you can choose whatever sort it is you wish to rear,
But if you want a clever one, they run a bit more dear.

They also have some special ones that don't look quite so nice,
But they can write the Lord's Prayer all on a grain of rice,
Or, if you are extremely rich, a Genius in Bud!
Guaranteed to think all day, and not play in the mud.

And if there is a local dialect you have to meet,
You can select a baby which will either cry or greet,
And if you do not want a child who might appear coarse,
Choose one from "Pass the Ketchup" and not from "Gis the sourse."

The shop lays down requirements which you will have to meet,
To keep the baby safe and give him what he likes to eat.
They'll reject your application if you are a person what'll
Holler at the baby and not sterilize his bottle.

But if you are admissable, then rush down to the Sales,
Pick one up at half the price and slap him on the scales
After Bottle Break when they're contented and replete,
At the Baby Shop, at the corner of the street.

I Fell for a
Black and White Minstrel

I fell for a black and white minstrel,
He tickled me under the chin,
What I wanted to say was 'You go away'
But I actually said 'Oh . . . come in'
In a minute I was captivated,
I had not a second to think,
What I could not erase, as I gazed in his face,
Was 'What does he look like . . . pink!'

We went to his lodgings in Clapham,
Ostensibly we went for tea,
Only I kept on sort of looking at him,
And he kept sort of looking at me,
And the thing with a black and white minstrel,
They're not like a man who is clean,
If you've covered your chest, with a pearly white vest,
You can very soon see where he's been.

He sang me 'Oh dem Golden Slippers!'
He danced me a pulsatin' dance,
With his muscular thighs, and his white-circled eyes,
A maiden like me stood no chance,
He flung off his gold lamé jacket,
And likewise his silver top hat,
He cared not a fig, as he tore off his wig,
And I'm telling you no more than that.

But too early the traffic grew louder,
And I knew that it had to be dawn,
I reached for me black and white minstrel,
But me black and white minstrel had gorn,
I sat all alone in the morning,
Not wanting to understand,
That I had been only a plaything,
I was only a pawn . . . in his hand.

To this day I still cherish the pillow,
Where my black and white minstrel did lie,
There was one little place, where he laid his black face,
And one where he laid his white eye,
Me black and white minstrel has left me,
Gorn! with never Goodbye,
But my heart will be with him in Clapham,
Till the waters of Swannee, run dry.

The Husband's Lament

or Well, You Certainly Proved Them Wrong

The flowers round our garden gate
Are strangled now with nettles,
The caterpillars got the leaves,
The road dust got the petals,
There's cracks across the asphalt path,
And the dusty wind do blow,
I know they say "domestic bliss",
But I dunno . . . .

There's trikes chucked on the garden
And there's writing on the wall,
The kids have smashed the wash house
With their little rubber ball.
The paint's peeled off the woodwork,
And the gutter's sagging fast,
I bodged it up last autumn,
But . . . it didn't last.

And in our shattered living room,
The telly's on the blink,
There's fag ends in the saucers,
And peelings in the sink,
There's holes burned in the carpet,
Where it smouldered half the night.
"A Woman's Work is Never Done"
And you certainly proved that right.

There's barnacles in the goldfish bowl
And curlers on the floor,
The budgie's out the window
And the woodworm's in the door.
The leaves fell off the rubber plant,
The leg fell off the bed,
The smiles fell off our faces
And the back fell off the shed.

And *you*, who I adored,
One look and I knew I was falling,
You stole away my heart,
Beneath the moon and that tarpaulin,
It *can't* be you beside me,
With your tights so full of holes,
Chewing through your supper,
All them picalilli rolls.

We've been together twenty years today,
And there's a moral,
Since we have no conversation,
We have never had a quarrel,
We hardly see each other,
So we never have a fight,
For "Silence it is Golden"
And we've certainly proved that right.

Thank you and Good-night all you Winklepickers

I hate this buying shoes,
I do, I hate it with a passion.
Whatever else I wear,
Me shoes are always out of fashion.
And that's because my feet
Are everything I'd wish they're not,
They're long and wide and knobbly
And usually they're hot.

Oh, curse them winklepickers!
All turned up at the ends,
That I used to cram me feet in
To go dancing with my friends.
I'd cut the light fantastic
With a face so grim and sour,
And when I took them off,
I'd sit and laugh for half an hour.

Who *invented* winklepickers?
It's his fault that nowadays
When I stroll along,
Me feet are pointing different ways.
I read that Chinese ladies
Bound their feet up to the knees,
And they're welcome, if they like,
But then they're clever, these Chinese.

Whatever else I might be,
Indecisive I am not,
It's wellies when it's raining,
And plimsolls when it's hot.
I'm not saying that I have no shoes,
That statement would be wrong,
It's just I have to find one
That's as broad as it is long.

When I shop for shoes
I come up flapping in me daps,
And they show me little shoes
With just a tracery of straps.
And as I stuff me foot in,
And the leather starts to crack,
I see the place is empty,
'Cause they're laughing round the back.

In the hope of dainty footwear,
I'll continue with the hunt,
Breathtaking in me slippers
With the pom pom on the front,
And the one thing on my mind,
As I go flapping down the street,
Is why don't I entitle this:
I Wish I'd Looked After Me Feet.

The Flit Gun

My Mother had a Flit Gun,
It was not devoid of charm,
A bit of Flit,
Shot out of it,
The rest shot up her arm.

The Wedding

Come sit beside me love, now that the lamps are burning low,
We'll gaze upon our wedding cake lit softly in the glow.
Oh, it was a lovely one, with candles burning bright,
Not too hard or crumbly, Oh the texture was just right,
The icing was a masterpiece, the marzipan was soft,
The effigy of you and me both standing up aloft,
Don't hesitate to take some if I've tempted you enough,
It's marvellous. And someone ought to eat the bloody stuff.

And draped along the sofa is my lovely wedding gown,
Rented for a tenner from the other side of town,
With graceful sleeves of satin and the collar edged with lace,
Skilfully designed to softly frame my smilin' face,
With lovely sprigs of blossom where the cuff laid on my hand
Which I had shyly offered to accept the wedding band,
The stately train which swept the aisle and floated all about
To hopefully conceal the fact that I am growing stout.

And stuffed there in a jam jar, my unblemished bride's bouquet,
With lovely ferns and lilies that entwine and fall away,
From scented stephanotis and a shy and rambling rose,
Set among the tendrils and the pastel satin bows.
I clutched it to my bosom as my love and I were wed,
That over my abdomen all the fronds should softly spread,
For though I knew the frontal view was just a blushing bride,
My shape I fear did not appear too hot viewed from the side.

And you, my love, with whom I shall withstand life's stormy weather,
Despite the fact we haven't got two pence to rub together,
Smile up at me from where you are prostrate upon the floor,
Still groggy from the stag night you arranged the night before,
And smile on us, Good Fortune, may our mighty mortgage shrink,
Keep us off Security, the panel and the drink,
Keep my stranglehold full on the gizzard of the purse,
As we travel on life's journey – for better or for worse.

The Vegetable Garden and the Runaway Horse

In everybody's garden now
The grass has started growing.
Gardeners, they are gardening,
And mowers . . . they are mowing.
Compost heaps are rotting down,
And bonfires burning low,
So I took up me shovel,
And resolved to have a go.

I dug a patch of garden
That was not too hot or shady,
And not too large to tax
The constitution of a lady.
Everything which crossed my spade,
I flung it all asunder,
And that which I could not dig up,
I rapidly dug under.

And in my little plot,
I bravely laboured with the hoe,
Enthusiasm running rife,
I sprinted to and fro.
I stopped for nothing,
Not for food or drink or idle words,
Except a spotted dick
Someone had chucked out for the birds.

Imagine then my pleasure,
As it all came sprouting out,
I cast aside me dibber
And I swaggered round about,
But, alas, the gate
To which my garden was adjacent
Was open, and I never saw,
As up the path I hastent.*

*sorry folks

86

When I went down on Saturday,
A horse stood in my plot,
But nothing else stood in it,
For he'd eaten all the lot.
I said, "Alas, my effort's wasted
And my garden wrecked.
Go away, you rotten horse,"
(Or words to that effect).

His hooves had crushed me lettuce,
And me radishes were mangled,
Broken canes were scattered
Where me runner beans had dangled.
The lovely shiny marrow
I'd been going to stuff and all,
The horse had broke it off its stalk,
and kicked it up the wall.

Standing in the ruins
Of me Brussels sprouts and spinach,
I threw away me shovel
And I said, "Well, that's the finich.
No early peas for me,
The birds can have them,
Or the mice might,
And if I want a cabbage,
Well, I'll see you down at Pricerite!"

The Annual Holiday

or Will that Old Army Suitcase Hold out Another Year Dad?

Well, I'm off on me holidays,
It's all within me reach,
I've got myself in trim,
For carting deckchairs round the beach,
With me flask of tea and cup,
I shall be pouring out the dregs,
With wasps all round me orange,
And with tar all round me legs.

All bundled up with cardigans,
(The weather's on the change)
I won't have slept the night before,
(The beds were all so strange)
I'll lay out on the beach,
Oh so remote and deeply tanned,
With me sandwiches, me knickers,
And me ears full up with sand.

At night, as we're on holiday,
It's on the town we'll go,
With sausages, chips and marrowfats,
At a couple of quid a throw,
And when we've spent our cash,
We'll wander home as best we can,
All along the Mini Golf,
To the smell of the hot dog man.

Or seeing as it's raining,
We'll pop out for a jar,
When we've fought the other tourists,
For a second at the bar,
We'll ignore those folks who've just come in,
Whose shoulders are so sore,
'Cause *last* week was so hot,
They couldn't step outside the door.

And then we'll travel home,
All sat religiously apart,
So we don't touch each others legs,
And make the sunburn smart,
With suitcasefuls of rock,
So everybody gets a stick,
And our hearts down in our flip flops,
See you next year. Kiss me quick.

Foolish Brother Luke

And as the cock crew, brave undaunted sound,
Rocks, from off his head, were seen to bound,
And at the hour of dawn by luck or fluke
Arose the form of Foolish Brother Luke.

Now Foolish Brother Luke, he had no sense,
He never listened to his good parents,
But places rough and low would oft frequent,
On alcohol and sordid pleasure bent.

One day, alas, he met his Waterloo,
For Luke he had no sense like me or you,
There he sat upon his own dustbin,
Eatin' a banana, in its skin.

Sittin' on a bin across the road,
There lounged the form of Schemin' Annie Toad,
She knew he had some money, 'cause she'd seen
Him in the dirty places where he'd been.

Pattin' all her curlers into place,
And rubbin' cochineal upon her face,
She crossed the road to Luke and said, "How do,
Foolish Brother Luke, I fancy you."

He choked on his banana, and he fell
From off his bin a-cryin', "Bloody Hell!
At last it's happened, like I knew it would,
Come inside and have some . . . Christmas Pud!"

For Foolish Brother Luke was not so soft.
He'd pondered long up in his bedroom loft,
He knew *she* had some money, 'cause he'd seen
Her, in the dirty places where she'd been.

But what Luke did not know, poor foolish lad,
Annie Toad was mistress to his Dad,
What Annie did not know, by luck or fluke,
Was that her Mum was not averse to Luke.

Annie Toad had blackmailed poor Luke's Dad
To name her in his will and so he had,
But Luke to Annie's Mum had done the same,
So who, or why, or what was there to blame?

And so they wed, the gay misguided pair,
Throwin' all their money in the air,
But yet, a word of warnin' needed here,
They were struck by lightning.

The Secretary's Song

Secretary is my trade,
Shorthand typist, second grade,
With me pad clutched in me hand a
Living breathing memoranda.
Like a ramrod on the seat,
I will sit up straight and neat.
With me feet placed close together,
I'll remark upon the weather,
But don't ask me more than that,
Because I haven't got the brain
To respond.

I find when seated in my chair,
With my conscientious stare,
Stabbing pains come in me eye for
What you write, I can't decipher.
But when I rush in with the teas,
I'll charm the birds right off the trees,
I'll run to do the washing up
And pick the fag ends out the cup
Until I hear the siren blow,
Then I'll just clock my card and go
Home.

I will not appear to choke
In conferences thick with smoke.
In vain I'll write the boring minute,
And assume some interest in it.
I won't elaborate the facts,
And I won't come to work in slacks
For they offend the royal eyeball
And that cannot be allowed at all,
For what's the point of women
If you cannot see their legs?

And when at last I'm seated by
The great typewriter in the sky,
Let me type the letters right,
In the morning and at night.
Let the Snopake grow on trees,
Let men's hands stay off me knees,
Let it be a place harmonic,
With no need for gin and tonic.
Thank you in anticipation
Of your favourable reply,
Craving your indulgence,
Yours sincerely.
Good-bye.

Oh Don't Sell our Edgar no more Violins

Oh don't sell our Edgar no more violins,
That dear little laddie of mine,
Though he's but eight, we'd prefer him to wait,
Or I doubt if he'll live to be nine,
He plays the same song, and it's sad, and it's long,
And when Edgar reaches the end,
With his face full of woe, he just rosins the bow,
And starts it all over again.

Now Daddy says Edgar's a right little gem,
It's only Daddy's *face* that looks bored,
It's really delight, makes his face appear white,
When Edgar scrapes out that first chord,
Daddy of course, he was filled with remorse,
When Edgar came home from the choir,
To find that his fiddle, well, the sides and the middle,
Were stuffed down the back of the fire.

So don't sell our Edgar no more violins,
When next he appears in your shop,
His Daddy and me, we are forced to agree,
His fiddlin' will soon have to stop,
Sell him a clean, or a filthy magazine,
Ply him with whisky or gin,
A teddy! A bunny! or just pinch the kids money,
But don't sell our Edgar no more violins.

For though it be a mortal sin,
We'll do the little fiddler in,
Don't sell our Edgar no more violins.

I Don't Want to go to School Mum

I don't want to go to school Mum
I want to stay at home with my duck.
I'd rather stay at home with you Mum,
And hit the skirting board with my truck.
Don't make me go to school today Mum,
I'll sit here quiet on the stairs
Or I'll sit underneath the table
Scratching all the varnish off the chairs.

I don't want to go to school Mum
When I could be underneath your feet.
It's shopping day and we could go together
Taking twice as long to get to Regent Street.
And every time you stop to talk to someone
I won't let you concentrate, no fear,
I'll be jumping up and down beside you
Shouting "Can I have some sweets Mum?" in your ear.

Or how about me doing a bit of painting?
Or what about a bit of cutting out?
Or sitting in the open bedroom window
Body in and legs sticking out?
Or what about us going up the park Mum?
Or how about me sitting at the sink?
Or what about me making you a cake Mum?
And Mum. Hey Mum. Mum can I have a drink?

And Mum, Mum what's that at the bottom of the cupboard?
And Mum, what's in that bag you put down there?
And hey Mum watch me jump straight off the sofa,
And Mum, whose dog is that stood over there?
What you doing Mum? Peeling potatoes?
Sit me on the drainer watching you
I wouldn't *mind* me trousers getting wet Mum.
Oh I aren't half fed up. What can I do?

What time is Daddy coming home Mum?
What's in that long packet? Sausagemeat?
How long is it before he comes Mum?
And Mum. Hey Mum. What can I have to eat?
Oh sorry Mum! I've upset me Ribena.
Oh look! It's making quite a little pool.
Hey Mum, hey, where we going in such a hurry?
Oh Mum! Hey Mum, you're taking me to SCHOOL!

Puppy Problems

I bought myself a puppy
And I hoped in time he might
Become my friend and ward off
Things that go bump in the night
So I put him in a shoe box
And at home I took him out
And then began to learn
What owning puppies is about

I tried so hard to love him
And I didn't rave or shout
As he bit into the sofa
And he dragged the stuffing out
I *gave* him things to chew
But soon I couldn't fail to see
That he liked the things he *found*
More than the things supplied by me.

He frayed my lovely carpet
That I'd saved my pennies for
And when he wasn't chewing
He was weeing on the floor,
Nor did he spare the table leg
That came in for a gnaw
Though I told him off the message
Never seemed to reach his jaw.

We laboured at the gardening,
Me and my little pup
At two I planted flowers
And at four he dug them up
He liked to dig, he'd bury bones
And pat it down so neat
And then he'd rush indoors
As clods of mud flew off his feet.

I bought a book on training
And I read it all one night
And when we set off out
I really thought we'd got it right
With titbits in my coat
To give him once he got the knack
But he didn't so I couldn't
So *I* ate them coming back.

When I commanded 'Heel!'
He never seemed to take the point
But galloped on half-strangled
Tugging my arm out of joint
He jumped up people's clothes,
The cleaning bills I had to pay!
And when I shouted 'Here!'
He turned and ran the other way.

One day I drove him over
And I gave him to my Dad
Who welcomed him and trained him
But it left me very sad
So I thought I'd let you know
In case a pups in store for you
That its very wise indeed
To have a Dad who likes dogs too.

Clive the Fearless Birdman

Clive the fearless birdman was convinced that he could fly,
At night he lay in bed and dreamed of soaring through the sky
Of cruising through the clouds, of winging far out into space
And he had a leather helmet with a beak stuck on the face.

Clive the fearless birdman had a wife who did not care,
For his fly by night ambition of cavorting through the air,
With mocking and with ridicule she did her best to kill it,
And cruelly filled his breakfast plate with cuttlefish and millet.

But in his little potting shed he'd built some mighty wings,
Out of balsa wood and sticky tape and plasticine and strings,
Up to his neck in feathers which had taken months to pluck
He laboured with his Evo-Stick, he fashioned and he stuck.

He tried it on at last and slowly turned from side to side
So wonderful was it that Clive the birdman slumped and cried,
So shiny were the feathers all in silver grey and black,
With eiderdown all up the front and turkey down the back.

It strapped on with a harness buckled round his arms and throat,
All made adjustable to fit the thickness of his coat,
Just to see him walking in the street made women shriek
As he flapped by in his harness and his helmet and his beak.

So Clive announced to all the culmination of his search
And told the local papers he'd be jumping off the church
Seth the old gravedigger with his face as black as coal
Said 'If he jumps off the steeple I shan't have to dig a hole'.

And so the day arrived and all the people came to stare
Police held back the crowds and all the local press was there
Clive read out a noble speech, an address to the people
That nobody could hear for it was windy up the steeple.

He stepped out in the sky and flapped his wings just for a minute,
Far above the vicars garden as he plummeted straight in it
He lay there in the cabbages without another flutter
And the beak came off his helmet and went rolling in the gutter.

But far away in Heaven Clive the birdman reigns supreme
Soaring through the air without the aid of jet or steam
So at the Pearly Gates if its with Clive you wish to speak
You can tell him by his harness and his helmet and his beak.

Will anybody Marry me?

Will anybody marry me?
I would not cost him dear
I am in perfect nick
And good condition for the year
He would not have to be a Mr. World
Built like Fort Knox
For I would do the plastering
And saw up all the blocks.

Will anybody marry me?
I would be awful sweet
I'd let him knock me glasses off
And kick them down the street
And I would not be a nagger
Saying 'Will you paint the pelmet?'
And if he was a fireman
I would never dent his helmet.

And concerning older girls
Our inhibitions have all gone
And me dad's an electrician
So I'd really turn him on
Now I cannot give my telephone
That's hazardous I know
But if anyone will have me
It is Bognor 410.

HAIR — INEXPENSIVE TO MAINTAIN BUT NOT YET GREY.

BRAIN ... YES.

NOSE — ARISTOCRATIC, UP-TURNED IDEALLY SUITED FOR HAVING A GOOD SNIFF.

RURAL VOICE ... REMINISCENT OF EARLY SPRING MORNINGS WITH FINGERS OF MIST ON THE GRASS, JEWELLED COBWEBS, STEAMING DUNGHEAPS ETC.

CHIN — FIRST OF MANY.

BONY ELBOWS FOR SUGGESTIVE NUDGING.

DIMPLES IN ALL OF THE RIGHT PLACES.

HARD-WORKING HANDS (HAVE BEEN KNOWN TO WRITE).

EARS — PIERCED FOR IMPROVED REAR VISION.

EYES — GUARANTEED NOT TO TAX A MAN'S INTELLIGENCE.

SMILE — A RUSH OF TEETH TO THE MOUTH.

SHOULDERS — DEVELOPING NICELY.

HEART ... LOTS OF.

CHILD-BEARING HIPS (PROMISE OF FRUITFULNESS).

KNUCKLES — CRACKLING WITH HEALTHY YOUNG ARTHRITIS.

DELICATE ALMOND-SHAPED FINGERNAILS ON WHITLOW-FREE HANDS.

KNEES — SHAPELY (HAVE BEEN KNOWN TO DRIVE MEN INSANE).

ELASTIC STOCKINGS NOT REQUIRED (YET).

HUGE FEET FOR GREATER STABILITY. (DOUBLE STAMPS ON TUESDAYS)

* LARGE FEET RUN IN THE FAMILY.

GENUINE ONE ONLY
PAM AYRES
1947 MODEL
SPORTING SPECIFICATION
GOOD RUNNER
(Poetry in motion!)
HOUSE-TRAINED ● FRIENDLY
GOOD WITH ANIMALS & CHILDREN
Complete with Accessories
NO REASONABLE OFFER REFUSED

Bournemouth

He was long and tall and thin and dull
And so was she,
He dried his trim moustache
When they had drunk their China tea.
And he was very quiet, very rich
And rather kind,
With one eye that could see
And with the other, which was blind.

His hair was rather sandy
And his manner rather terse,
His clothes were very dull and safe
But then, well, so were hers.
Her shoes were very dear
And never purchased on a whim,
They toned in with the wardrobe
And it was the same with him.

She couldn't really claim,
That as he read the *Business News*
And regaled her now and then
With his opinions and views,
That his figure was endearing
In the fat expensive chair,
Flecked about with dandruff
From his thin and sandy hair.

And neither in his heart
Could he blossom and rejoice
To listen to her speaking
In her flat and toneless voice,
To watch her rosebud mouth
Which would habitually melt
Into a little smile
She always smiled but never felt.

But they got along together
And they liked the same shampoo,
And he was so polite
With "Oh dear lady: After you!"
And when they walked on Sunday
He would always take her hand
And hold it like a cold dead fish
Washed up along the strand.

Most weekends you could see him
Striding out across the links
While she would be presiding
By the double drainer sinks,
Concocting gourmet meals
But ritualistic, free of mirth,
Rosé and white and lobster bright
And things that cost the earth.

And as she whipped the cream
And folded in a little more,
She saw the dark-eyed sailors
As they lingered on the shore.
And he sat on the verandah
With his *Telegraph* and *Punch*
And watched the young girls laughing
As he waited for his lunch.

Ever since I had me Op

Hello, it's nice to see you looking well,
What? How am I?
I haven't been so good myself
But I've been getting by
Yes, I've had a bit of trouble
Well, I wouldn't bore a friend
But if you knew how much I'd suffered
Well, your hair would stand on end.

No, I'm not one to complain
And we all have our cross to bear
And I wouldn't even tell you
What they did to me up there
If you asked how many stitches
I wouldn't let it cross me lips
Well alright then, twenty seven
And that's not including clips.

Course, it was only fifty fifty
On the drip all night and day
Oh they gave me all the lot
And then they took it all away
You wouldn't have recognised me
And I'm glad I never seen ya
And the doctor on the case
Gave up and went back home. To Kenya.

Well, I know you're in a hurry
And you haven't time to stop
And I've just seen Deirdre
She'll want to know about me op
And there's always someone worse off
Than yourself, without a doubt,
In my case I haven't met him
But I'm sure that he's about.

And you're healthy dear, enjoy it
For it fades away so soon,
Now I've got me eighteen pills
So I'll get through this afternoon
Don't give a thought to how I've suffered
I'm the last one to complain
And I'll keep on smiling through it all
Until we meet again.

107

The Dreadful Accident
with the Kitchen Scissors

I gave my lovely teddy bear a haircut,
For Mother she had sent me for a trim
And really, I felt that much better for it
I thought that I would do the same for him.
I picked him up and grabbed the kitchen scissors,
"Just a snip or two old bear," I said,
But I find I was not cut out as a barber,
For accidentally, I tore his head.

I do not criticize the man who stuffed him,
He had to do it thoroughly no doubt,
But I wish he had not stuffed the head so solid
Then I could stop the stuffing coming out.
I've had to wrap me bear's head in a turban
Well, he's been dressed up like it for a week.
Mum asked me, "What's he got that round his head for?"
I said: "He's a bus conductor . . . he's a Sikh!"

But how long can I keep up the deception?
Where his face was plump it's sunken in
And though he's very hard across the forehead
He's turning very soft around the chin!
I haven't dared to look beneath his turban,
I know it's just a mass of coloured foam,
And Mother's started looking very puzzled
As she picks up bits of it around the home.

And Auntie Greta's coming here for dinner
And she's the one who gave the bear to me
And that is when my crime will be uncovered
For I know that he won't stand much scrutiny.
Oh Mother, Auntie Greta, I'm so sorry!
I *tried* to sew his head up, I tried hard!
But as I said, they stuffed his head so tightly
That every stitch has stretched out half a yard!

I'm waiting by the door for Auntie Greta,
I rammed poor Teddy underneath the quilt,
And every time a car stops by our gateway
Both me knees start knocking from the guilt.
She's bound to say, "Now where's that lovely Teddy?"
And his head's all caving in . . . What shall I *do*?
Oh Crikey, here it is, a blue Marina . . .
Oh, Hello Auntie Greta . . . how are you?

Thoughts of a Late-Night Knitter

I had a lovely boyfriend,
Knit one, purl one.
Had him for a long time,
Cast on for the back.
Had him all the summer,
Loved him, cuddled him,
Push it up the knitting pin
And gather up the slack.

Well he *knew* how much I liked him,
Knit one, purl one.
I made him seven jerseys,
Never did him any wrong,
And he told me that he loved me,
Knit one, purl one.
Told me that he loved me
But he didn't stop for long.

Well he never said he'd left me,
Knit one, purl one.
He never even told me
'Cause I found out on me own.
I was going up the chippie,
Knit one, purl one.
And he came out of the pictures
With that horrid Mary Stone.

Well I didn't know what hit me,
Knit one, slip one.
After I'd looked after him
It wasn't very nice,
And they went off down the High Street,
Laughin', gigglin',
And left me on the corner
With me chips as cold as ice.

Well it isn't that I miss him
Knit one, drop one.
I never even think of him
Good riddance . . . ta ta!
I'm very independent!
Snap one, tie one.
I've never been so cheerful,
Ha ha . . . ha!

And I hear they're getting married,
Knit one, drop nine.
I wish them every happiness,
It's *lovely* staying in!
Well I don't need romancing,
Cuddlin', dancin'.
Bundle up the knitting bag
And sling it in the bin.

Rocking Gran Blues

Who says I'm too old for the disco?
While the music still touches me soul,
While I dance in bare feet and move with the beat
And me feet turn as black as the coal.
Oh just say the word, young Adonis!
I'll reggae with you till it's day,
Just lend me a fag and pass us me bag
For me Pan Stick has all run away.

Oh yes, I know you've seen nothing like it!
My dancing is lissom and free!
Take a look round the place, each wondering face,
Everyone's looking at me!
Oh take it away, lay it on me!
We'll tear up the floor through the night,
We'll be rocking and reeling while the ball on the ceiling
Festoons us in speckles of light.

I've scraped all me hair in a beehive,
I've stapled it up at the back,
Though once it was pepper and salt, dear,
Now it is ebony black.
Tell the deejay to turn up the volume!
Turn it up with no fear of reproof!
So we hear the pound and the pulsating sound
And the woodworm all fall out the roof.

For there's nothing like music to get you,
Oh the shivers it sends down your back,
And if you're approaching the bar, dear,
I'll have a nice rum and black.
And get me a packet of crisps, dear,
Bacon or onion will do
And then *mon amour* we'll give it what for
And dance till our faces turn blue.

And then in my clapped out Ford Consul,
Parked by a rippling stream,
I'll flash you a smile, find the spot on the dial
And cover the windows with steam.
It's the wonderful weekend for working,
So until Monday when we clock on
Take my hand in the dark, out in the car park
It's Saturday evening: rock on.

After the Jubilee

Don't play anything else on your squeeze box Mother
To Honour the Jubilee.
I daresay the Queen would enjoy it
But it has started grating on me.
Come and sit on this tattered old bunting,
Here's your tea in a Jubilee cup,
Don't play "God save the Queen" for a minute
Or in other words Mother . . . shut up.

Ah but how we rose to the occasion
With our patriotism and flags,
With our parties and fêtes and processions
And our Jubilee carrier bags.
How we planned for the local street party
With the sun beating down on your head,
But unfortunately it rained on you and me
So we had it in Angus's shed.

But the dingy old street, how we decked it,
How the neighbours all clattered and talked
As they knocked the tin tacks in the Union Jacks
And the next day the whole lot had walked,
And the kiddies all rushed down to help us,
Who's to say industry never pays?
They wrote, "Long may she reign" on the brickwork
And it did look, it poured down for days!

And the bonfires they lit in the village,
Well, we'll see nothing like it again,
And the only bonfire that burned brighter
Was the shock one up Arsonists Lane.
And we went on a torchlight procession,
We all bought special torches for that.
I held mine up high, proudly up in the sky,
And me shoulders got covered in fat.

So before you strike up again Mother
Let me refill your Jubilee cup.
Me slab cake went down in the middle
But I've turned it the other way up.
The fireworks and fêtes are all over,
The street parties swept up and done.
Here's a message for Buckingham Palace,
Can we do it again? It was *fun*!

Little Nigel Gnasher

Little Nigel Gnasher was his name,
He bit his nails.
When other boys were having fights
Or finding slugs and snails,
You always knew that Nigel
Would be at his normal station,
Beside the rails he bit his nails
Eyes shut for concentration.

His mother tried to stop him
But young Nigel's ears were shut.
She wrapped his hands in woolly gloves,
But Nigel Gnasher cut
Straight through the woolly fabric
With his sharp and practised teeth
And bit the helpless fingernails
That sheltered underneath.

Mrs Gnasher took him
To the Doctor one fine day.
The Doctor looked at Nigel's nails
And quickly looked away,
Saying, "Calcium deficiency
Has laid these nails to waste."
And he gave the lad a bag of chalk
But he didn't like the taste.

Oh he bit them on the landing
And he bit them on the stair.
Nigel Gnasher bit his nails
Till there was nothing there.
Nigel Gnasher bit them
Till he couldn't stand the pain
And then he'd summon up his courage
And bite them all again.

When other people rested
Hands outstretched on the settee,
Nigel sat upon his hands
So people wouldn't see.
He plastered them with Dettol,
Savlon, Germolene and more,
He'd have it done by half past one
And bite it off by four.

One day a local millionaire
Was driving round about.
He spotted Nigel Gnasher
And impulsively leaned out
Crying, "Here's a present, sonny,
From eccentric Jeffrey Krupp,"
And a fiver hit the ground,
But Nigel *couldn't pick it up*!

And then the local bully,
Carver Clay, he came along
And though his head was short,
His fingernails were very long.
He pushed aside poor Nigel
Who lay clawing at the ground
And ran off with the fiver
Shouting, "Look what I have found!"

So the moral of this story,
Little Gnashers far and wide,
Is, don't bite them up the middle
And don't bite them down the side,
Don't bite them front or sideways,
Spare your poor nails from the habit,
Then if someone throws a fiver
They will be on hand to grab it!

A Tale of Two Settees

It was down at the furniture warehouse,
As I wandered one morning in May,
To buy a settee for the woodworm
Had eaten me old one away.
It was there in a flash that I saw him
In front of the chipboard veneer.
His Levis and shirt were covered in dirt
And he had a gold stud, in his ear.

I did not let on that I'd seen him
Oh no, for I played hard to get,
Deliberating by the vinyl
And stroking the uncut moquette.
But he casually walked over to me
And seductively murmured, "Oi, Oi,"
And there in the furniture warehouse
I said, "Well . . . you are a tall boy!"

He said, "Can I be of assistance?
Or offer a little advice?
Now if it's a sofa you're after
Well, this one's especially nice,
Upholstered in sultry black leather
And done round the edges in chrome,
And I know it withstands shocking treatment
For I happen to have one at home."

Oh I know it was wrong but I liked him;
I knew he would lead me astray.
And yet as the sun caught his earring
I heard myself saying, "Okay."
When he asked me to go to the pictures
And ignoring the customers' glares
I said, "Is it Studio One then or Two?"
He said, "Studio Three. That's upstairs."

So I met him that Saturday evening
I went all dressed up in me prime.
He brought me a fragile white orchid
And a drink on a stick at half time.
He bought me a carton of popcorn
Our eyes met as I prised up the lid.
"Oh thank you," I said to him softly
And he laughed and said, "Stick with me . . . kid."

We went for a Chinese and there in the dark
To the clang of the Chinese top ten,
"Your beauty," he said, "has gone to my head
With the sweet and sour pork." Oh and then
He said, "Darlin' it's wrong, but I'll ask you,
Oh, make all my cravings complete,
Instead of just buying a sofa
Why don't you invest in a suite?"

Clamp the Mighty Limpet

I am Clamp the Mighty Limpet
I am solid, I am stuck,
I am welded to the rockface
With my superhuman suck.
I live along the waterline
And in the dreary caves.
I am Clamp the Mighty Limpet!
I am Ruler of the Waves.

What care I for the shingle,
For the dragging of the tide,
With my unrelenting sucker
And my granite underside?
There's only one reward
For those who come to prise at me
And that's to watch their fingernails
As they go floating out to sea.

Don't upset *me*, I'm a limpet,
Though it's plankton I devour.
Be very, very careful
I can move an inch an hour!
Don't you poke or prod me
For I warn you – if you do
You stand there for a fortnight
And I might be stuck on you!

The Slimming Poem

I'm a slimmer by trade, I'm frequently weighed,
I'm slim as a reed in the river.
I'm slender and lean, and hungry and mean –
Have some water, it's good for your liver.

Don't give me cheese rolls or profiteroles,
Don't show me that jelly a-shakin',
Don't give me cream crackers, you picnic and snackers
Or great big ice-creams with a flake in.

Don't give me swiss roll or toad-in-the-hole,
Don't show me that Black Forest gateau.
You sit and go mouldy you old garibaldi
Your pastry all riddled with fat. Oh!

When I'm fat I feel weary and tubby and dreary
The stairs make me struggle and grunt dear,
And yet I'm so happy and punchy and snappy
When me hip bones are stuck out the front dear.

No, it's white fish for me, no milk in me tea
And if we don't like it we lump it,
No figs or sultanas, no mashed-up bananas,
No pleasure and no buttered crumpet.

So don't get any bigger, me old pear-shaped figure
I can and I will become thinner.
So cheer up and take heart, pass the calorie chart,
Let's see what we're having for dinner!

Take me back to old Littlehampton

I didn't *want* to come on holiday
I know I shan't enjoy it.
If I think of any way to hamper yours
Then I'll employ it.
I didn't like the journey
And I don't like our hotel
And I wish I'd stayed at home
That would have done me very well.

No! I am *not* going swimming,
Not with my infected ear,
Not with all those half-dressed women
Running up and down, no fear.
I'll just sit here in the bedroom
Oh and pull the curtains, do
For the sun inflames me headache.
Oh it's all very well for you!

You go and have a lovely time
Don't think of me at all.
No, I've got me English paper
You go out and have a ball,
You go and have a rave up!
Go on! Go and have a fling!
But don't come for me at dinner time,
I couldn't eat a thing.

Last night I ate that gastro-enteritis on a plate.
I thought I'd make it to the Ladies'
But no, I was too late.
Go on! Enjoy your dinner!
Have the fish oil and the wine!
But buy some Alka Seltzer:
I shan't give you one of mine!

I could have been at home now
Sitting watching the TV
With me hair all washed and set
And with the cat sat on me knee.
I can't use me heated rollers
For the volts are up the creek
And the bath's full of sand –
I haven't had one for a week!

Still, it's all right, no it's lovely,
And we saved up for a year.
Dear Mother, having a lovely time
I wish that you were here.
How I let myself be talked
Into a fortnight I dunno,
Still you go out – enjoy it!
One week down. And one to go.

The Stanford Mafia

Oh I'm tired of pushing a pen
And writing poems round the place.
I think I'll have a change
And undergo a *volte-face*.
On considering the choice
Of an alternative career
What I'd most like to be
Is a protection racketeer.

I wouldn't want to do it
In the city or the town
For that is trespassing in gangland
And I s'pect I'd get mown down.
No I'd stay out in the country
It's where I prefer to be.
I'm your friendly neighbourhood mugger
In your area - fly me.

We would not be extortionate
At all you understand,
But me and Angel Face Scarlatti'd
Sort of amble round the land
Saying, "We haven't come to murder you
Or worry you or con ya!
No, we're just passing through
We've come to put the finger on ya!"

I'd see that Mrs Lilly Sprocket –
Now I happen to know she knits
Oh the usual things, the bonnets
And the booties and the mitts –
Saying, "I don't want no trouble Lilly,
Trouble? Me? Bless your old soul!
But how much *is* it worth
To see your Knitmaster stay whole?

There's a lovely market garden
Up the road at Rushy Weir,
We could go and case the joint
And say, "Nice place you got down here."
I could take along a breeze block
Which I casually could toss
Straight through the greenhouse roof
To help the message get across.

We could go and see the farmer
With his golden fields of grain.
"Wotto me dear," I'd say
"I see we haven't had much rain.
I run a little service,
Dunno what you'd think it's worth,
I go round dousing people's blowlamps
If they've come to scorch your earth."

A protection racketeer!
Me brim turned down about me eyes,
I'd drive a mighty Buick
And I'd say, "Okay you guys,"
I'd puff me old cheroot,
Turn up me collar past me ear
This is Pam Ayres of the underworld!
. . . Nice place you got down here . . . .

The Car Wash
Black and Blues

Oh Dad, oh please don't send me down the Car Wash
Just like you send me every Friday night,
For on seeing the mechanical contrivance
I find that I am overcome with fright.
I put my fifty pence into the slot, Dad,
And as the mechanism starts to go,
The last thing that I see before the darkness
Is the wash attendant saying, "Cheerio."

And it's black, Dad, black as night inside the Car Wash,
And every time I realize too late
That the wireless aerial's not in the socket
And before my eyes it scribes a figure eight.
I know it's quick, Dad, speedy and efficient,
Them brushes clean the car from head to feet
But they also get the windscreen wipers, Daddy
And flick them half a mile across the street.

Them rubbers, Dad, they're slapping at the window;
I know they're supposed to make the paintwork gleam
But I am thinking Dad in all the racket
Will anybody *hear* me when I scream?
It's proper claustrophobic in the Car Wash,
Them brushes, Dad, are sinister and black.
If the front one doesn't lift the lid and get you,
Another one is rolling up the back.

You haven't got a coward for a son, Dad,
For all the times my back you've gaily slapped,
It's just that with the Car Wash coming at me
I sort of get the feeling that I'm trapped.
And all that drumming Dad, it isn't water
It's hot wax spraying all around the place;
One day I left the quarterlight ajar, Dad
And hot wax spattered all across my face.

Oh, Dad, don't let us patronize the Car Wash
Let us go back to our old-fashioned plan,
Washing it ourselves on Sunday morning
With a squirt of Fairy Liquid in the can.
Don't send me down the Car Wash any more, Dad,
Send my sister, send my cousin Alf,
Send someone insensitive and stupid
Or alternatively, drive it there yourself!

In 1978, the Health and Safety Executive launched a campaign aimed at reducing the number of injuries sustained by children playing on building sites. I was sent a horrific list of accidents which had befallen these children and I was asked to contribute something in verse form to the campaign. This was my reason for writing "Building Sites Bite!"

Building Sites Bite!

This is a horror story
And it's worse because it's true.
Dan Sandheap and Fred the Hole
Have come to talk to you,
Claude the concrete mixer,
Mick the Brick and Cable Man
Have come here from a building site
To warn you if they can.

Claude the concrete mixer
Came up shuffling to the front.
He said, "All day on building sites
It's back and forth I shunt.
The workmen prop me up
And rush away to eat their lunch,
So you play under me
So I can fall upon you . . . CRUNCH!"

Fred the Hole spoke up,
His voice as deep as any grave,
"Climb in me one rainy day
And down the walls will cave!
I'll trap you in the bottom
Where no one can hear you shout
Or see you in the mud and muck
Nor run to get you out."

Dan the sandheap piped up with,
"They think they're at the sea
When they spy my lovely sand,
They run and climb on me
And then I tumble down on them,
All slippery and seething.
I cover them in sand and soon
I can't feel any breathing . . . ."

For building sites are dangerous –
Great lorries rush about
And just one lick from Mick the Brick
Is sure to knock you out.
Cable Man said, "I'm just one
Bare wire here alone
But touch me with your fingers
And I'll burn you skin and bone."

On building sites these rotten creatures live
And many more,
So please don't *play* on building sites
It's not what they are for.
They're full of danger everywhere
Scattered all about.
Too many children venture in
And never come back out.

The Wasp he is a Nasty One

The wasp he is a nasty one
He scavenges and thrives,
Unlike the honest honey bee
He doesn't care for hives.
He builds his waxy nest
Then brings his mates from near and far
To sneak in your house
When you have left the door ajar.

Then sniffing round for jam he goes
In every pot and packet,
Buzzing round the kitchen
In his black and yellow jacket.
If with a rolled-up paper
He should spot you creeping near
He will do a backward somersault
And sting you on the ear!

You never know with wasps,
You can't relax, not for a minute.
Whatever you pick up – Look Out!
A wasp might still be in it.
You never even know
If there's a wasp against your chest,
For wasps are very fond
Of getting folded in your vest.

And he *always* comes in summer.
In the wintertime he's gone
When you never go on picnics
And you've put a jersey on.
I mean what other single comment
Causes panic and despair
Like someone saying, "Keep still!
There's a wasp caught in your hair!"

But in a speeding car
He finds his favourite abode.
He likes poor Dad to swat like mad
And veer across the road.
He likes to watch Dad's face
As all the kids begin to shout,
"Dad! I don't like wasps!
Oh where's he gone, Dad? Get him *out*!"

And I'd like to make a reference
To all the men who say,
"Don't antagonize it
And the wasp will go away,"
For I've done a little survey
To see if it will or won't,
And they sting you if you hit them
And they sting you if you don't.

As we step into the sunshine
Through the summers and the springs,
Carrying our cardigans
And nursing all our stings,
I often wonder, reaching for the blue bag
Just once more,
If all things have a purpose
What on earth can *wasps* be for?

133

The Railway Carriage Couple

Our home's a railway carriage
And it cannot be denied
That you might describe our dwelling
As a little bit on the side
Yet it has the odd advantages
Where other housing fails
And we're on the straight and narrow
So we can't go off the rails!

Our decor is original
Its simple but it's good
With little plaques screwed on the wall
That give the type of wood
And up above the headrest
Of the seat marked number five
Is a photograph of Cheddar Gorge
In case we don't arrive

Yes we're the railway carriage couple
With the long drive at the front
Or it might be at the back
If we feel like a change, and shunt
We're a little isolated
But if ever I get bored
And feel like communicating
I stand up and pull the cord

I don't do much entertaining,
It's too cramped, you see, by far
For dining graciously
Because it's not a buffet car,
So we eat out in the corridor,
My husband doesn't care
But I like to face the engine
Even though it isn't there.

Of course there is a certain problem
Which we have and always will
In that we cannot use the toilet
While the train is standing still
So we built one just beside us
And we glazed it in with glass
The first time my husband used it
He came back and said 'First Class!'

We have a little garden
We don't buy much in the town
You can see us any evening
Raking clinker up and down
You might see us in our door
If you don't travel by too fast
And we'll let down two holes in the leather strap
And wave as you go past.

Oh love, you got no poke left
I didn't want to say,
It seems we are outmoded,
Much too slow, and in the way.
You know how much I love you;
I'd repair you in a flash
But I haven't got the knowledge
And I haven't got the cash.

There is rust all round your headlamps,
I could push through if I tried.
My pot of paint can't cure it
'Cause it's from the other side.
All along your sides and middle
You are turning rusty brown,
Though you took me ninety thousand miles
And never let me down.

Not the snapping of a fan belt
Nor the blowing of a tyre
Nor the rattling of a tappet
And nor did you misfire.
All your wheels stayed on the corners
And your wipers on the screen
Though I didn't do much for you
And I never kept you clean.

All your seats are upholstered
And foam rubber specks the floor.
You were hit by something else once
And I cannot shut the door.
But it's not those things that grieve me
Or the money that I spent,
For you were my First-driven,
Ninety thousand miles we went.

I could buy a bright and new car
And go tearing round the town
A BGT! A Morgan!
(With the hood all battened down).
But as I leave you in the scrapyard,
Bangers piled up to the skies,
Why do your rusty headlamps
Look like sad, reproachful eyes?

Good-bye Worn Out Morris 1000

Ned Sails in the Sunset

Don't play me them nostalgic ballads, Eunice,
You know it breaks my aching heart in two,
You know it makes me think of darlin' Neddy
And how such men are far between . . . and few.
I still can see him standing on the quayside,
In his uniform and all, he looked so grand
With gold braid gleaming all around his helmet
And a cornish pastie steaming in his hand.

"Good-bye my love!" he cried, his throat constricted,
"You are my comfort and my sustenance!"
He faltered and I thought emotion choked him
But he'd tried to eat the pastie all at once.
I held him and beseeched him, "Sail in safety!
Journey through the darkness to the light!
May Providence protect your tattered rigging
And hold your rudder steady in the night!"

He turned to board the craft, my heart was aching,
Crying, "Ned . . . shall I never see you any more?"
But he brushed away the salt spray from his eyebrow
And resolutely shut the cabin door.
I watched his boat sail off into the sunset,
A thousand violins began to play,
And I thought I saw an old tomato sandwich
Tossing back and forth among the spray.

A mile off the shore the fog came down to shroud him,
It hid the Channel Ferry from his view,
It sliced his boat in half, the back and front end
And Ned was standing in between the two.
They sent the air-sea rescue out to find him
But just a cornish pastie stayed afloat.
Don't play me them nostalgic ballads Eunice
For Ned and I are severed . . . like his boat.

A-3

Driving in London's my pleasure
I prize it above any other.
One hand on the wheel,
The fingers like steel,
And the *A–Z* clenched
In the other.

The Music...

The Secretary's Song

With resignation:

Se-cre—ta-ry   is my trade Short-hand

ty-pist se-cond grade With me pad clutch'd in me

hand a Liv-ing breathing memor-an-da —— Like a

ram-rod on the seat   I   will   sit up straight and

neat With me feet placed close together I'll remark upon the

wea–ther—— But don't ask me more than that B'cause I

hav-en't got the brain———— To re–spond.——

Oh Don't Sell our Edgar no more Violins

With quiet desperation:

Oh don't sell our Ed-gar no more vi-o-lins That dear lit-tle lad-die of mine— Tho' he's but eight we'd prefer him to wait— Or I doubt if he'll live— to be nine— He plays the same song— and it's sad— and it's long— And when Ed-gar reach-es the end——— With his face full of woe he just ro—sins the bow— And starts it all o—ver—a—gain.